REFLECTING STRENGTHS

35 REFLECTIONS ON THE ART OF FOSTERING RESILIENCE IN OUR CHILDREN - AND OURSELVES

SECOND EDITION, 2025

CHRIS TROUT

Published in 2025 by Lead Differently LLC

South Portland, Maine

ISBN 979-8-218-59412-1

printed in the united states of america

cover design by Zoe Trout,

based on original image:

ID 5895209 © Mike Monahan | Dreamstime.com

To Alex and Zoe, my most patient, wise,

and demanding teachers

and most inspiring role models,

and to Suzanne, my quiet

foundation, my joy,

my home.

To my friend and teacher Misty Stenslie, a joyful warrior who transformed unfathomable adversity to live a life of courage, generosity, and joy.

ACKNOWLEDGMENTS

My first acknowledgment must go to the **Alberta Home Visitation Network Association** (AHVNA) in Edmonton, Canada, for they are the reason you hold this book in your hand. Allow me to explain...

It has been nearly 18 years since I first published *Reflecting Strengths*. As I pursued opportunities to explore a strengths-focused perspective in leadership and personal development, I allowed the first edition to go out of print.

Much to my surprise, that little collection of stories from 2006 was still alive and well in Alberta, Canada! When the AHVNA reached out to ask if I happened to have 100 copies still lying around for their use, I decided it was time (the perfect time, actually) to breathe new life into both the book and workbook with an update of the original stories and the addition of 14 new reflections.

That's the way life works sometimes, and I am deeply grateful to my Canadian friends for this accidental reminder that this work is still relevant in 2025.

I would also like to express my deepest gratitude to:

Pepper Jackson, for your exquisite and insightful personal story, *Mommy, are we poor?*

James Trout, for *The missing piece,* your inspiring personal story about a teacher who changed the trajectory of your life — and to Mrs. Bergeron, whose alternate mirror changed everything.

Zoe Trout, *Zoe Trout Creative Strategies,* for your patience, skill, and superb taste in designing the cover for the second edition.

Theresa Tillman, for your invaluable suggestions as a proofreader. What a marvelous gift you were!

Suzanne Drown Trout, my beautiful wife, for your quiet yet powerful support, always.

My readers, seekers all, who breathe life into these words.

And the thousands of **young people and caring adults** who have graced my life and informed this work. You are the true teachers.

THANK YOU

"We can only be said to be alive in those moments when our hearts are conscious of our treasures."
~ Thornton Wilder

CONTENTS

HOW TO USE THIS BOOK

What do you mean, "use this book?" Can't I just read it and enjoy the stories?

You sure can! They will inspire you, intrigue you, and sometimes challenge you. That's enough.

For those who want to explore these ideas more deeply, I've provided a few additional tools.

At the end of each chapter is a brief set of questions and/or exercises titled ***reflect...*** where you will find one or more of the following kinds of prompts:

- ***you***: These are designed to help you reflect on your own experience, both as an adult and when you were a child.
- ***them***: These are designed to help you reflect on the young people in your life and the transformative role you can play in their unfolding stories.
- ***try this***: These exercises will challenge you to put insight into action.

Using these prompts, you can level up your exploration by:

- Incorporating them into your daily meditation or study
- Reading the book with a colleague or friend and letting the questions serve as fodder for conversation.
- Sharing the stories in your staff meetings or parent group to trigger a discussion and explore the ideas further.

I want more...

After the publication of the first edition, many of you asked for ways to explore strengths-focused thinking more deeply, both individually and in educational and staff development settings. For you, I have designed ***Reflecting Strengths: The Workbook***.

With hundreds of questions, exercises, and discussion prompts — as well as supplemental teaching materials — this workbook is designed to be used in conjunction with the *Reflecting Strengths*. While the core exercises in the Workbook correlate directly to the original 21 reflections in this book, I have also included additional exercises and reflections to enhance your learning.

Reflecting Strengths: The Workbook can be ordered at Amazon.com. Requests for discounted bulk orders may be sent to chris@leaddifferently.com.

Enjoy!

INTRODUCTION

"The light in their eyes."

These were the words that echoed through me when, as a blessedly naïve nineteen-year-old, I first began to work with children and youth who experienced the world through the lens of adversity: autism, behavior "disorders," substance abuse, abandonment, or any of the myriad insidious circumstances that cause us to be seen as broken and in need of repair.

From the beginning, I had little interest in their diagnoses or labels. All I could see was that inner light that cried out to be seen and named. The deep sense of admiration and wonder it evoked in me sparked a lifelong commitment to reach through the fog, meet them halfway, and give them a glimpse of the strength and beauty I could see — in hopes they might see it, too.

But they lived in a world that was too often blind to their strengths, mirroring only their perceived (albeit significant) deficits.

Could we — the caring adults in their lives — offer an "alternate mirror" — a version of themselves that includes the amazing strengths they used every day just to survive? And could they learn to use these very strengths to thrive?

Countless times over the years, I began my journey with a young person with some version of the words:

"I see the light in your eyes. There's something strong and powerful inside you. Don't let go of it. It will see you through."

Often, this was met with a quiet stillness that let me know I had pierced the armor. They likely doubted the truth of what I had said, but the directness of this statement conveyed what we all long to hear: *"I see you."*

To be clear, this is not an act of faith, but rather an act of perception. We don't have to believe — the evidence is already there. We are simply the messengers and the mirrors, standing in awe and sharing what we see.

Nearly fifty years and countless stories later, this is what I know for sure: There is a resilient light that burns in all of us, and we long to see it reflected in the eyes of someone we trust — that we might come to see ourselves strong, resilient, and able.

I am deeply indebted to the research pioneers who also saw that light and have studied it with such rigor and care. While their insights have informed what follows, this book is in no way an accounting of that knowledge.

Instead, it is a personal collection of stories, lessons, and insights grounded in my day-to-day search for that light. I share them not as an expert but as a fellow traveler, striving to understand the remarkable power of knowing and living from our strengths.

Beginning with an inspired lesson from "foster kids" (and some giant sequoias) and ending with the little miracles buried in my own journey, this collection explores ideas ranging from the power of intention and perception to self-image, resilience, the language of strengths, giving ourselves a break, *and* the power of one.

In my ideal world, these reflections will raise as many questions as they answer and challenge as many ideas as they affirm. For my desire is to start a conversation, not have the last word.

Whether you are a parent (in all its varied forms), teacher, mentor, or one of the thousands of professionals who support youth and families, my hope is that you will see yourself – as well as the young people in your life – in these reflections.

May they affirm what you've known to be true and give you courage and confidence that even the smallest interactions can ignite transformation and you needn't get it "right" all the time. By simply choosing to look for the light in their eyes, you already change how they see themselves in yours.

For this, we know for sure...

Where we focus, grows.

Chris Trout, 2025
South Portland, Maine

1

BRING IT ON!

One hot July, I spent a week in the mountains with kids in the foster care system. I learned about the strengths that grow from adversity and the power of resilience. And every day I grieved for these kids — for the roots they lacked and the security they longed for.

During a break one morning, I had the transformative experience of touching a giant Sequoia. It measured thirty-nine feet across at its base, reached three hundred feet into the sky, and had been standing in that spot for over two thousand years.

My mind exploded, barely able to contain my awe. Imagine what this magnificent tree had survived, I thought. Drought? Floods? Winds? Fire?

How had it survived?

Then I learned that the roots of this ancient being, one of the largest and oldest on the face of the earth, reached no deeper than five feet into the ground. Five feet! How could it possibly stand so tall and survive so long with such a seemingly weak root system?

How, indeed. For it turns out that same root system stretched out over an acre of land, intertwining with the roots of dozens of other Sequoias to need one another and hold each other up. It literally balanced on the breadth, not the depth, of its foundation.

How ironic that I had this experience while in the presence of young people who had been torn from their own roots, often over and over again. Most had faced unimaginable adversity, and each carried the scars of loss and isolation.

Yet, every one of these young people carried a light in their eyes that evoked awe and wonder. They taught me what resilience looks like: how the leanest protective factors — a neighbor, a good friend, a caring adult long since past — have the power to cushion the "damage" and stoke that inner light.

They taught *me* to teach *them* about the breadth of their roots – all the people who care so deeply about their well-being, even in a system that seems determined to fracture those connections. They taught *me* to teach *them* about the strengths they had used to survive – the very strengths that could help them thrive.

One moment crystallized this learning for me. During a presentation that afternoon, I wrapped a young girl in several colorful jackets, each symbolizing a protective strength she carried inside her: the humor from her gramma, who died when she was six; the courage she gained from a long-past neighbor who told her she was smart; the quiet persistence that had carried her through so many foster homes. As she stood there, wrapped in the comforting layers, I turned to the group and said, *"There may even come a time when you look out at the world that has dealt you this hand and say, 'Bring it on! I can take it!'"*

The group fell silent. The air was electric. They knew this truth. They had railed at the gods.

Now, they were getting it. They could feel their roots reaching out to one another — a community of peers who had something powerful that those enviable kids with "perfect" families did not: the strengths to take on the world and the knowledge that they could endure, survive, and thrive.

It was a privilege to stand with these young human Sequoias as they allowed this truth to seep into their very beings. They taught me where resilience lives and how it comes alive.

They gave me courage.

They gave me hope.

Bring it on!

reflect...

you: As a young person, did your roots run deep or broad? Who were the important people in that root system? What did they do, or what characteristics did they have, that made them valuable to you?

Do you have that feeling that you can survive any adversity that comes your way? If so, how do you know this? What are the strengths that served you before that you believe you could count on again? (Humor? Perseverance? Positive outlook? Faith? Insight? Adaptability? Tenacity?)

If not, think about the challenges you have faced, even if they don't feel as dramatic or "important" as the ones in this story. What personal characteristics got you through them? What relationships, objects, places, or beliefs helped you survive?

them: How do you anchor the young people in your life so they can grow?

How do you see the young people in your life reaching out to extend *their* root systems? Who are they reaching out to — and how? Have you labeled some of these new roots "bad" or "dysfunctional" (gangs, the wrong crowd, sexual partners, etc.)? What can you teach this young person about themselves that might impact where those roots find fertile ground?

How do you anchor the young people in your life so they can grow?

try this: Make a list of the characteristics inside you and the circumstances around you that have helped you face adversity. Give them specific names like perseverance, humor, self-restraint, adaptability, and so on. Now, say or write a phrase that simply says this: "I am _____" or "I am a person of _____." Write or say this phrase for as many characteristics as you are able to name.

Now, look in the mirror: allow yourself to speak these words:

Bring it on!

2

MOMMY, ARE WE POOR?

I am deeply grateful to Pepper Jackson, one of the brightest, most loving, and resilient souls I've had the privilege to meet along my path, for sharing this exquisite and personal story. Used with permission.

I t was a "poor me" day.

My husband had traded me in for a younger model and left me with three young boys. Child support was spotty, at best, and my three jobs certainly weren't covering all our needs.

On this particular evening, I had dragged home a broken pallet from our local grocery store to burn in our living room fireplace so we had some heat. My tears were just below the surface twenty-four hours a day. Then, my youngest asked the dreaded question.

"Mommy, are we poor?"

My pride kicked in. I laughed and asked, *"Sweetie, do you think we're poor?"*

He thought for a minute and admitted he wasn't sure, but some kids at school had told him he was.

Summoning every ounce of strength I had, I looked him in the eyes and said, *"Honey, poor is a state of mind."*

"I bet your classmates aren't camping in their living room or toasting marshmallows in the fireplace. I bet they aren't sharing funny stories and laughing themselves to sleep in their sleeping bags on a Tuesday night."

That night, I made a promise to my sons: we were going to look at our situation as an adventure.

We moved the table out of the breakfast nook and replaced it with the couch. Every night, as I cooked their dinner, they would sprawl across our crazy "couch in the kitchen" and do homework as we engaged in a daily ritual called "Hi-Low." Each of us would share a high moment of our day and a low moment. We processed our days together — as a unit.

As they grew, each child explored their own hobbies and paid for their own interests. My oldest loved golf. We certainly couldn't afford golf lessons or even clubs, but he got a job working at a golf course, became a scratch-golfer, pursued a degree in golf course management (on scholarship), worked for several PGA courses, and has caddied for celebrities and professionals alike.

He's now pursuing a law degree.

I invested everything I could in experiences for them. They went to a private school (I was "that woman" who cleaned the church every week in exchange for financial aid). They went on class trips. My oldest spent a year studying in

England and traveled through Europe by train. My middle son took a year off to teach chemistry in Egypt.

Today, all three are educated, independent adults — and so much fun to hang out with.

How? Why? It came down to a change of attitude — the decision to embrace exactly what we had — and make it awesome.

It wasn't always pretty, and some may count the ways we failed. But we chose — we chose to see every "failure" as the opportunity for an adventure.

This was our chosen life...

strong, resilient, together.

reflect...

you: How do you think you would have responded to this child's question: *"Are we poor?"* What situations have you experienced in your life where you had to make a quick decision about how to see something, so someone else could see it differently too?

them: Do you think this family's story would have unfolded in a different way if Pepper had responded differently in this moment? And how did this moment shape everything that came after? What question would you want to ask Pepper if you could talk to her about this story?

try this: Think about an everyday moment in your life that shaped who you are: something someone said or did. How do you wish it had been different? How do you imagine your story might have changed as a result?

3

HARRY POTTER LEARNS THE TRUTH

There's a powerful scene near the end of the final *Harry Potter* movie that speaks a simple but profound truth. Harry has "died" and finds himself in a place of white light, speaking with his old mentor, Dumbledore. As their conversation draws to a close, Harry faces a decision: return to physical life or remain in the spirit world. As Dumbledore walks away, Harry calls out to him and asks (paraphrasing here),

"May I ask you a question, sir? All of this — is it real or is it just in my mind?"

Dumbledore smiles wryly and replies, *"Of course it's in your mind, Harry. But why would you think that's not real?"*

Perfect.

I saw this play out time and again during my years working with "high-risk" teens. If they saw themselves as stupid, troubled, or failing — labels that matched the external reality they (and most others) perceived — that is exactly the reality they lived out every day. But if they began to recognize the extraordinary strengths they used every day just to survive, and experienced *that* as the essence of who they really were — strong, resilient, resourceful, and wise beyond their years — they would begin to live a very different reality.

Reality, it turns out, was entirely in their heads. It was just a matter of choosing a different reality than the one agreed upon by everyone else.

And here's the powerful part: Internal reality, when consistent and strong, always wins.

This same truth drives all those dramatic, "against the odds" stories we love in books and movies. The hero never beats the odds because of what they do (though it seems that way). They triumph because they can imagine a reality no one else sees, before anyone else can see it.

Where others see financial ruin, the hero sees opportunity. Where others see imminent death, the hero sees life.

The same is true for you.

If you look at your life and conclude that you are overwhelmed, financially inept, hopelessly overweight, unlovable, or not good enough, you will most *certainly* find a ready and willing match for that reality. Reinterpret the same data while acknowledging your strengths, persistence, caring, and growing wisdom and you will begin to create — in a million ways you couldn't manage if you wanted to — a very new reality.

Yes, it's all in your head. But don't think for a minute that doesn't make it real.

It is, in fact, the only thing that ever is.

reflect...

you: Imagine that, like Harry, you are standing in the white light asking someone you trust if the life you experienced was real or all in your head. What aspects of your life experience might be in question? And how would you interpret Dumbledore's answer?

What shift in your mindset (what's "in your head") do you believe would positively impact your life?

them: Think about a young person in your life. What do you see them creating through their thoughts and perceptions? How is it like or different from your reflections above — not in terms of content, but in terms of your ability to shift that internal reality?

Now, how is your internal "reality" influencing the way you engage with this young person?

try this: The temptation is to have a conversation with your young person about the way they think about their life. Instead, challenge and play with your own perceptions about *them*. How might shifting the way you think about them help you create a new reality?

4

YOUR BEAUTIFUL CHILDREN

Each June, I attend a most remarkable dance recital. It's remarkable because the teacher doesn't really teach dance — though there sure is a lot of beautiful dancing going on!

She teaches joy. She teaches comfort in one's own body and the celebration of creativity and self-expression.

And she doesn't so much organize a dance recital as an extraordinary celebration of children. The hundreds of family members who fill the auditorium are, of course, delighted to see their children and grandchildren, nieces and nephews, but something more is happening: This is an annual ritual celebrating each and every spirit that dances across the stage.

At the beginning of the show, the teacher invites us to see our beautiful children through her eyes – and we accept the invitation.

For the next two hours we watch children of every age, every shape, every demeanor, engaged in pure delight. Not once do I see the over-serious, self-conscious, anxiety-ridden faces associated with "recitals." These children and young people are engaged in fun – and are allowing us to peek in.

With each joyful performance, the audience roars its approval with whoops and whistles. We're seeing these beautiful children – all of them – through the teacher's eyes.

Make no mistake, these children have worked hard and are proud, but somehow it's the joy and delight that shines through most powerfully.

What's the teacher's secret? How does she accomplish this remarkable feat?

I suspect she sees every one of these kids as genuinely beautiful. She doesn't appear to be concerned with other people's expectations — what a dance class "should" look like or whether parents will measure their investment by the perfection of form or the height of a leap. She's clear on what she believes is most important and keeps her focus there.

And because she does, these children and teens have the opportunity to see their beautiful selves through her eyes.

What do the young people in your life see in *your* eyes?

———

reflect...

you: What was your feeling reaction to this story? Was it positive? Pollyanna? Negative? Were there any "yeah, buts?"

Did you feel hopeful and excited or did you think of all the reasons this couldn't happen in *your* situation?

try this: Describe, in detail, what your parenting or youth work would look like if you focused only on what was best for the young people in your life and didn't care how it was judged by others. What would this look like? How is it different from what's happening now? What fears or perceived realities prevent this vision from happening?

What would the young people in your life see in your eyes if this vision became reality? List three things you could do now (regardless of any barriers) to help ensure that they see this reflection in your eyes.

5

TREAT ME 'AS IF'

As I scanned the teen center, there they were: four of the toughest, most unyielding and challenging kids in town — huddled over a board game and looking for all the world like a bunch of light-hearted childhood friends, playing together without a care in the world.

Just ten minutes earlier, I had listened as a young girl in foster care, in a rare moment of vulnerability and hope, shared her dream. Her biological mom had just gotten out of treatment, and Mia was daring to believe this time would be different. She imagined her mom, sober for good this time, calling to say she had gotten a job and an apartment, and wanted Mia to come live with her — to start over again, just the two of them.

Time and again, I've witnessed this extraordinary duality in young people who have faced far too many challenges with far too little support. Hope and fear live side by side with equal intensity — a rock-hard exterior occasionally giving way to gut-wrenching vulnerability.

As caring adults, we are, at first, deeply touched by these profoundly paradoxical moments, then overwhelmed by the magnitude of "issues" that prevent these moments from lasting longer. We are frustrated by their seemingly endless poor decisions — and awestruck by their sheer will to survive. So, in our overwhelm, we focus on the "issues" and get about the business of fixing them.

But here's our paradox: Our true power lies in doing the opposite.

When we acknowledge the "issues" but choose to speak to the hope, vulnerability, and strength, we send a different message. We communicate that what's *right* about this young person is more powerful than what's wrong, that their strengths can help them overcome the adversity in their lives.

It's not easy. After all, the hard stuff dominates how we see these kids. But that's *their* norm, as well. Hundreds of times each day they are reminded that their issues = who they are.

Who are they to disagree?

Yet, once they have shown us their hope, vulnerability, or strengths — no matter how briefly — we have the opportunity to relate to them as hopeful, open, and strong individuals.

Each time we do this, we offer them a glimpse of who they are reflected in a different mirror, an alternate mirror.

And as they catch sight of this reflection, they can risk exploring and exposing this part of themselves just a little more. And a little more... And a little more...

reflect...

you: Bring to mind one aspect of yourself that few people know and you rarely expose. Perhaps it's a silent love of singing, a seldom-seen wry sense of humor, or an unrealized longing to travel the world.

Now, imagine that someone you respect and whose opinion you value looks right past the "you" that you show the world each day and speaks directly to this hidden aspect of yourself – as if that's who you are: the singer, the comic, the wanderer. Close your eyes and imagine it. Notice the feelings. That's how powerful you can be in the life of a young person.

them: Have you ever witnessed this paradox? What did it look like? What were the overwhelming "issues" that you found yourself focusing on? What were the vulnerabilities and strengths that were evident? Describe what it would look and sound like if you looked right past these issues and spoke to the hopeful, open, strong child underneath. What would you say?

Describe what it would feel like (to you) to do this?

try this: The next time you interact with this young person, bring this picture – and these feelings – to the very front of your mind. Notice how this little shift changes your interaction.

Write down what you noticed and stick it in a place where you will see it when you are most frustrated by their behavior or decisions.

6

IF YOU KNEW THEIR SUCCESS STORY

I once moderated a panel discussion with five young adult alumni of the foster care system. Each had a remarkable story to tell — from addiction to heroin at birth to the search for a home that would welcome all five siblings together.

Each story of struggle and pain had a surprise ending, from *"I am valedictorian of my class"* to *"I will soon give birth to my first daughter."* The audience of therapeutic foster parents sat in awe of their courage and was filled with hope from their stories.

It was easy to identify the incredible strengths each of these young people had used to survive and thrive: raw humor and keen insight for one, the engaging smile and personality of another, a young man whose quiet assurance grounded everything he said.

But I wondered if these same strengths had been as obvious when they were younger. Had the humor been heard as cynical sarcasm? Did adults interpret the sunny outlook or quietness as a mask for deep hurt or anger?

I began to think about the flip side of the labels we use. How many are matters of interpretation: *Obstinate or persistent? Conniving or resourceful? Stubborn or determined? Annoying or passionate? Bossy or assertive?*

Of course, we can be — and often are — both. The question is: when kids are both, which label do we use? Which label helps them see their particular characteristics as potential assets?

It was no surprise to learn that, somewhere along the way, every single one of the young people on this panel had lived with foster parents who chose their labels carefully. They were persistent and tenacious about teaching their "chosen" children the strongest parts of themselves. They simply would not give up! Day after day, in words and, more importantly, in action, these parents methodically taught their children to see themselves through the lens of their strengths vs their deficits.

I stress their persistence because these children had not made it easy. They had felt the sting of negative labels and often struck back at a world that had rejected them. I have no doubt that there were many moments when these parents had reacted out of anger, frustration, and hopelessness.

Then, they took a breath or got a good night's sleep, and came at it again, knowing these children were counting on them to hold them in a different light — no matter what.

So, perhaps when you are at your wit's end and blinded by the cluster of hurt and harm, you can imagine a future time, when the child in your life is on stage telling the remarkable story of how they survived and thrived.

"How did you do it?" the audience will ask.

And they will point to the strengths they learned from you. And they will speak with awe about how you saw those strengths long before they could — and wouldn't give up. These children are worthy of your awe and admiration now. And it is you they will name as the transformative force who taught them who they are.

reflect...

you: Were there any labels that others used to describe you growing up that you now recognize as early indicators of strengths that have helped you navigate life? How would your journey have been different if those had been labeled as potential strengths instead of deficits?

them: *Can you imagine the young people in your life sitting on stage talking about their successes? What do you see in them now that might allow them to become the person on that stage?*

try this: Think about one or more young people in your life. What are the labels that you or others use to describe them — including when they are frustrating, annoying, self-destructive, etc. Can you identify the strengths version of those labels: obstinate vs persistent, conniving vs resourceful, stubborn vs determined, annoying vs passionate, bossy vs assertive? Remember that you can recognize and honor those strengths while still holding them accountable. Just remember that *where you focus, grows.*

7

IT TAKES TIME TO CHANGE MY MIND

As much as we love to imagine that our self-image is self-created, the truth is this: Much of how we see ourselves depends on how we see ourselves reflected in others.

If people roll their eyes every time I speak, it's not long before I perceive my opinions as "lame" or "stupid." If boys talk to me, but look at my friend, I learn that I'm "nice," but they are "pretty." And if adults label me "at-risk," then pile on platitudes, advice, and programs, I get it that I'm not seen as worthy of a genuine relationship – only techniques aimed at "fixing" me.

But when an adult looks me in the eyes, is genuine in *both* kindness and anger, and knows me well enough to name my strengths (even the hidden or misdirected ones), I begin to know that I'm worthy.

Now, I know for you, as an adult, my behavior can be confusing. My eyes may be diverted, and I might deflect your kindness with sarcasm or shrug off your anger as if it means nothing. I may even dismiss your recognition of my strengths as though you said nothing at all.

But know this: I need you to keep being the adult. Keep respecting me, telling me, standing with me. I need to know that *you* understand I can't let you in all at once.

When you keep teaching me about my strengths — not idealized ones you *wish* I had, but the ones you actually see in me — and when you keep telling me that you believe in me, it will get through.

And if you're paying attention, you'll see little clues that you're getting in: I'll hang around after everyone else has left, hoping to hear more. I'll show you that strength again — to see if you notice, again. I'll comment on others' strengths, so you know I've been listening. I'll "blow it" on purpose, just to see if you still believe in me.

Go ahead, hold me accountable. Just don't give up on me; don't stop seeing me.

I've been staring at the same at-risk, loser, failure, street-wise reflection for a long time. The reflection you're offering feels foreign and uncomfortable.

But I'll get used to it. I'll start to notice your version of me more often, and slowly, over time, it will tell me who I am. *Drip, drip, drip,* I'll begin to see myself as you see me: survivor, prevailer, person of strength.

And I'll begin to live as that person — and believe they are me.

reflect...

you: What did you see and hear mirrored back to you when you were a teenager — from parents, teachers, and peers?

What were the names and labels you gave yourself or others gave you? Which of these do you continue to own today, and which have you let go? What new names and labels have you taken on for yourself?

Was there someone along the way who mirrored back a different version of you — someone who seemed to see you and believe in you? Who was it? What did they do? What was it that allowed you to hear them?

them: What do you think I mean when I say "in both kindness and anger?" Is it OK to be/act angry with a young person? What are the boundaries and in what context?

try this: Think of one young person about whom you are particularly concerned or with whom you are particularly frustrated. What strong parts of them could you reflect back to them, and how? How could you reflect these parts in a way that might be heard? How would you know if your reflection "got through?"

Choose just one young person and, for one week, explore these questions until you feel you have an understanding of the answers. Imagine if you had this understanding for each young person in your life. *Imagine how powerful you can be.*

8

INCREDIBLY POWERFUL - AND
UTTERLY POWERLESS

Have you noticed this, too?

"Those kids" — the ones whose words, behaviors, and attitudes were most intractable — never did change because I figured out the right strategy, intervention, or perfect words. Before any of those mattered one bit, I first had to shift my focus and intent. If they did change, it was always because *something shifted in me first*.

Why? Because once I changed the way I saw them, they picked up on hundreds of nuanced shifts in my "vibe" long before I consciously *did* anything new.

I remember Ken, a 77-year-old volunteer I had in a teen center serving the roughest neighborhood in town. From the start, he was everyone's Grampa. All he had to do was sit on a bench. Within a couple of minutes, some kid would be sitting next to him, chatting away about nothing and everything.

Then, he got triggered. Ken simply could not bear watching them lie through their teeth when they were shooting pool or playing ping-pong. That was not the way he was raised and each time it happened, he got angrier and angrier.

He said nothing, but it wasn't long before he was sitting alone for his entire shift.

I knew I had to intervene quickly. I invited him into my office and let him rant about how wrong it was that we let them get away with this behavior. Then, I began to share some of their stories with him — stories of life on the street, substance abuse and violence in their homes, abandonment by the people they counted on most, and a world that labeled them as "trouble."

I asked how he might behave if, like them, he had never felt safe and lying to protect himself was all he'd ever known. How would he carry himself if his very survival depended on his ability to save face. Would he call that *mal*adaptive — or skillfully and necessarily adaptive? He admitted that he might behave much as they did.

"But how can they change if I don't tell them it's wrong?" he asked.

"If you were living their life," I responded, *"what do you think it might be like to have a secret 'Grampa' to talk to or just sit with quietly — a Grampa who didn't judge, but just loved you and made you feel safe?"*

Ken had had one of those when he was a child, and immediately understood what this meant to those hard-edged kids outside my office door.

He stood up, left my office, and took his seat on the bench. Within minutes, three tattooed, pierced, tough-looking "street kids" were standing around him, not always talking to him, but wanting to be near him. *What had changed?* Ken had done nothing differently — but the change inside him changed everything for those kids.

A few months later, during our regular check-ins, he reported there was not so much lying these days.

"That's you," I said. *"Oh, they no doubt still lie other places, but here, because of you, they feel safe enough to try something new."*

I've always found the idea that our perceptions hold so much power to be a bit unsettling. In fact, it seems almost grandiose to think that *our* perceptions are the key. Didn't we learn that the locus of control had to be with the individual, not with us? Isn't this what "empowerment" is all about?

This, however, is just one of the paradoxes we must accept if we are to be effective adults in the lives of young people who live in the midst of chaos, distrust, and unpredictability. *We are, at once, both enormously powerful and utterly powerless.*

Being an effective catalyst for change in a young person's life is, before all else, all about our intent. When our intent is clear and ego-free, the young person inevitably finds it easier to take the interpersonal risks that allow them to explore new ways of being.

At the same time, we have no ability to make them do what's right or healthy. The more we try to force that change, the less effective we become — often triggering the very behavior that triggered *us* in the first place.

If this sounds rather Zen-like, I suppose it is. When we can get clear on our intent – whether to *fix* them or stand with them as they find safety and new ways of seeing themselves in our presence — we become powerful *co*-creators in their lives, unattached to the outcome, but committed to their journey.

———————

reflect...

you: What was your reaction to this reflection? What parts challenged you, if any?

Does it make it easier or harder to know that your intentions have such a great impact?

What external pressures make it easier or harder to keep your intentions clear and ego-free? Are there situations where your own frustrations cloud your ability to stay clear on your intentions?

try this: Think of a young person in your life that truly makes you crazy (ie. annoyed, frustrated, angry, at the end of your rope). Jot down all of your intentions for being in this young person's life. How many of these have to do with fixing, changing, or stopping some behavior? (We're not debating whether accomplishing any of these might not be wonderful, just noticing the intention.) In the moment before you interact with this young person again, think to yourself, *"It's my intention to insightfully notice and teach this young person about their strengths so they can live from their strongest self. I can do this even while holding them accountable, keeping them (and myself) physically and emotionally safe, and being a consistent, trustworthy adult in their life."* Notice any changes in your energy as you interact or in the interaction itself. What do you want to remember about this experience?

9

AM I MY FATHER?

"Beauty is you not being afraid of who you are." ~ *Mary J. Blige*

One recent night, I got to visit with my dad. He died many years ago and has been mostly absent from my life since then, but he came to visit in a dream.

Now, before I tell you how that felt, let me first tell you who he was.

He ...

- *Could be a belligerent old cuss.*
- *Had a judgment, mostly a critical one, about nearly everything — and rarely left you guessing what that was.*
- *Neglected his health — and paid the price with a 25-year struggle with disabling heart disease.*

- *Had a great many inner demons that often bit him in the behind and undermined the success he longed for.*
- *Was terrible with money.*
- *Could be aloof and distant, more concerned with image than feelings.*
- *Sometimes behaved in ways that were less than admirable, and some of those hurt me in big, nasty, life-changing ways.*

He also...

- *Could be incredibly generous of spirit and, a couple of times when it really counted, was there for me.*
- *Was smart and articulate, insightful and sensitive, challenging and curious.*
- *Carried deep, secret desires for his life and, against all odds, stayed alive long enough to experience the ones that mattered most.*
- *Had a quiet gentleness and love of people that became more evident as he aged.*
- *Loved to tell stories.*
- *Loved life.*
- *Loved me.*

Yes, *all* of this is part of me. I am who I am because of the gifts *and* the struggles.

It's from him that I learned to write — *and* to struggle with money.

I inherited his love of life — *and* a penchant for judging it (and myself) too harshly.

He modeled loving others — *and* made it hard for me to love myself.

For *all* of this, I am deeply grateful.

As often as I've cursed the wounds of my childhood — and there were many — I could not see the world the way I do without those experiences. Don't get me wrong: I don't enjoy wrestling with his demons or working so hard just to accept my place on this earth, but I do enjoy being alive, aware, and able to articulate the lessons I am learning along the way.

That old cuss — that loving, paradoxical mess of a human being — courses through my veins.

And here's the best thing I've ever done (seriously, the best): I embraced it all. Both lists. Every bit of it.

For that was when I could finally move into the flow of my *own* life — and actually enjoy the ride.

So, I loved seeing my dad the other night. I woke up feeling gentle and satisfied. I missed him and wished we could have talked more. But there was no unfinished business.

And I was reminded once again:

My life is my own — that's the deal.

We're all here for the ride — the whole ride — and once we know that, all that is left to decide is whether we will be fully present for the experience: fearless, curious, and embracing it all.

reflect...

you: Do you have someone like my dad in your life — a paradox of deep hurt and moments of light? How much life energy do you spend cursing them or striving to be different than them? What would it be like to give up the battle and simply embrace it all, rooted in the knowledge that it has all contributed to the beautiful, strong, capable person you see in the mirror?

them: Can you imagine who these people are in the lives of the young people in your life? The alcoholic mother? The violent father? The stern, judgmental teacher? *You?*

try this: Ask one of the young people to tell you about their version of my dad. Don't interrupt, just listen, so they can tell you about all the parts: that fishing trip where they bonded *and* the stop at the bar on the way home, that one Christmas where everyone was on their best behavior *and* the next day, their longing for a different parent *and* their steadfast defense of the one they have. Just listen.

10

WHAT IF YOU DIDN'T KNOW MY PAST?

On a recent cross-country flight, I sat next to a delightful young woman, probably 17 or 18, headed for a summer visit with her East Coast parent. She was hard to miss with her lip and tongue piercings, tattoos, and hair that had clearly been through one too many color changes.

As we chatted, I learned just a bit of her story: parents divorced, high school on both coasts, classes at the local community college, etc.

What was more precious was what I didn't know. Was she a straight-A scholar with a rebellious streak? A "lost child" who skipped school, got in trouble with the law, and frustrated every adult who tried to help? An average kid who neither "lived up to her potential" nor caused much concern? Were the tattoos and hair just fun, or did it all have deeper meaning?

What a gift it was *not to know*.

We had delightful conversations about nothing and everything. She was at one moment articulate and engaging; the next, contradictory and bored. Without the baggage of her history, I could only relate to her at face value, offering her a mirror of herself that was untarnished by past choices or my interpretations of what those choices might mean.

She was free to explore new ways of being herself with me.

Isn't this one of the gifts we can offer the young people in our lives? The chance to start again? This is the opportunity we have each day with the young people in our lives.

I know it's not always easy, especially with teens who are labeled "difficult" and have grown accustomed to "being in trouble." It often took months of consistently starting fresh every day before they could accept that they truly had a clean slate each time they walked through the door.

Day after day, having held them accountable the previous day for some dangerous or unacceptable behavior, they'd walk in the door expecting me to still be "mad," to be holding a grudge. They would test me, checking to see if my "it's a new day" attitude was for real.

They were so used to being defined by past failures that they couldn't believe anyone would keep giving them the chance to be different.

But once they trusted this to be real, I could feel their relief as they began to share both their regrets and tentatively let me in on their aspirations.

In those moments, they gave me a profound opportunity: to see them not as stunted caricatures defined by negative labels, but as dynamic, evolving, paradoxical beings — just like me.

Their explorations were often slow and tentative. The old, negative mirrors in their lives still reflected who they *had* been, not who they were becoming. But slowly, the courage to explore a different self emerged.

And emerged.

And emerged.

---

reflect...

you: Have you ever gone to a new school, a new town, or a new workplace and dreamed of "starting over" so you could present a new and better version of yourself? How did this feel? What were your hopes? What were your fears?

Being able to start anew or try again, regardless of what has happened in the past, is one of the most powerful aspects of resilience-building relationships. Why do you think this is? Why's it so hard to do?

try this: The next time you are lost in the cycle of negativity with a young person, imagine that you are meeting them for the first time on a plane. They have no peers around, so they feel no need to save face. You have nothing to lose and no biases to feed. Nothing left to do but have a thoughtful, funny, insightful conversation with an interesting young person. Who are they now?

Picture them again on this flight. What would be your initial impressions? What might you end up talking about? What would it be like to relate to *this* version of them next time you interact?

This is a fun activity to role-play. Partner up and have one person role-play the identified young person on this flight. Let the rest of the group reflect on what they see and hear.

11

IF YOU ONLY KNEW WHY

Sometimes, wisdom and courage come in such unexpected packages – if we can only see them.

Jace provided very few reasons to like him. He was crass, angry, disrespectful, and constantly in conflict with every conceivable authority figure in his life: school, parents, police, neighbors. He seemed hell-bent on antagonizing everyone in his path.

The oldest of five children, each by a different father, Jace's "home" was a volatile mix of prostitution (his mother), drug dealing (her boyfriends), poverty, and neglect.

When I heard he had been in jail over the weekend, I wasn't surprised. He had vandalized someone's motorcycle – beat the crap out of it with a baseball bat, actually.

Probably drunk and showing off, I thought.

They slapped an electronic bracelet on his ankle and, until his court date, he was allowed to be at home (seriously?), school (again, seriously?), or at the teen center with me.

"Nice bling!" I said when he walked in the door. *"Tell me about it."*

For once, his bravado was gone as he began to tell his story. He had arrived home late Friday night and, standing in the kitchen with his mom, she announced that she was pregnant (again!) by yet another boyfriend — a well-known neighborhood drug dealer — who walked into the room just as Jace got the news.

Can you even begin to imagine Jace's rage — at his mom, at the boyfriend, at this life!?

I immediately understood. Reaching out, I shook his hand as he stared at me, bewildered at my response.

"Congratulations," I said. *"Extraordinary self-restraint. You wanted to beat him, didn't you?"*

Truth. As I suspected, the bike had belonged to the boyfriend.

In the face of his blinding rage, Jace — who I'd come to believe had little self-control and who I thought cared nothing about his future — had made a choice. Confronted with feelings he couldn't begin to understand, he had walked away, redirecting his rage to the bike instead of the man — and saving his own life in the doing.

I was immediately filled with respect and awe for this young man, who carried both love and deep anguish for each new baby born into the chaos of this family.

"Congratulations," I said. *"You are a person of incredible self-restraint."*

The impact of those words was clear in his eyes. He felt seen, known, and understood — perhaps the first time.

It didn't change the consequences of his actions – nor should it have. He was still responsible for the damage he had done.

But it did change the backdrop against which the rest of the story — and his life — unfolded. He began to see himself differently. In that alternate mirror, he was strong and caring, someone who mattered enough to make different choices, someone with self-restraint.

And now someone else knew, too.

---

reflect...

you: What was your reaction — your *gut* reaction — to my conversation with Jace?

Write about or discuss the range of reactions and concerns that come up for you. What fears or question marks come into your mind when you think of affirming someone who has engaged in behavior that's clearly wrong, destructive, even violent?

you: Imagine a time in your life when, despite your best intentions, you hurt another person — perhaps a spouse or friend or family member — in some way. Now imagine that, at the height of the fallout, someone you respected saw through your "bad" behavior and affirmed your intention: to protect, buy time to fix it, avoid embarrassment, absorb the consequences for someone else. Does it feel like that affirmation would excuse the harm you did or give you the strength to see a different solution? What if you were already being held accountable for your behavior? Does that make a difference?

Imagine that you were a known "screw-up" and always had been, and that others have stopped even expecting anything different. Every day, you wake up to those expectations.

Now imagine that one person, someone you respect and admire, congratulates you for a strength that you didn't even realize you had. How long would that comment stay with you? Would you remember it – even if you discounted it – the next time you were in a similar situation?

try this: If you have a young person in your life who fits this description, pay attention for the next week. Jot down notes when they do things that indicate caring, empathy, or other unexpected traits. Is any of their "negative" behavior an expression of these characteristics? Can you affirm their intention without affirming their behavior?

This is your challenge.

12

THE POWER OF 'AND'

"*My son disobeys me at every turn!*" insists Pam, an exasperated single mom. "*I don't know what to do. I don't feel like I can trust him anymore. I'm just at the end of my rope!*"

As her neighbor presses for specifics, Pam describes a litany of "just barely" breaches of her rules.

Curfew is 11:00 pm. "Josh" chronically calls at 11:15 to say he's sorry, where he is, and when he'll be home.

Josh knows he's not allowed to be home alone with his girlfriend. He tells his mom about having to stop by the house (with his girlfriend in tow) to pick up his homework, then staying for forty-five minutes because his friend was supposed to call with part of the assignment.

The rule is: No alcohol parties – ever. Josh tells Pam about a gathering that turned into a party when the soccer team arrived, keg in hand, to celebrate their big win. He hung out for a while, then left because "they're a bore."

Perhaps you're already shaking your head in recognition. Can't Pam see what a great kid she has? Josh is considerate and calls when he's late. He tells her about breaching rules, even when she might not have found out otherwise. And he appears to get out of situations he isn't supposed to be in.

"But he needs to call before he's going to be late… and curfew is 11:00, damn it!"

"But he's not supposed to be in the house with his girlfriend in the first place!"

"But he didn't leave right away – and he didn't leave because he should, only because he was bored!"

The word that gets us in trouble here is '**but**.' **But** invalidates anything that comes before it and focuses our attention (and commentary) exclusively on what's wrong.

But sets up absolutes.

But doesn't listen or notice or give partial credit.

But makes us crazy and takes us to the extreme, so we feel "exasperated" or "at the end of our rope."

Most harmful, **but** fails to distinguish between Josh and a kid who completely ignores curfew, sneaks behind Mom's back and hides it from her, or stays at the party to drink. And if we don't distinguish, Josh will eventually not distinguish either.

So what's the alternative? How do we hold Josh accountable and give him credit for his strengths?

The magic word is '**and**.'

And invites noticing: *"I appreciate that you called **and** we* *need to talk about curfew so I don't feel like you're playing games with me."*

And invites credit where credit is due: *"I really appreciate that you explained why your girlfriend was here. I get the fix you were in, **and** I really need you to respect my wishes and avoid getting in that fix in the first place."*

And invites validation and questions: *"I'm so glad you left the party **and** I'm wondering if boredom was the only reason you left?"*

"Mom! Give me a break! Of course not!"

When we shift our perspective to take in and acknowledge the *whole* picture, we shift the focus from "let me tell you what's wrong with you" to "let me tell you what I need from you."

Pretend for a moment that you screwed up or had bad judgment (not that this would ever happen!) and your boss, spouse, or friend is letting you know. What would work for *you?*

———

reflect...

you: Can you relate to Pam? In what way? What situations? Notice *all* that's true. What feelings come up when you think about these situations?

try this: For each of the above, write an accurate statement of what's true. Sit with a partner and let them reflect back to you what they see and hear as true.

try this: When do you use the word *but*? List some examples. Is there a correlation between the depth of your emotions about the situation (out of control, angry, frustrated, scared, anxious) and your use of the word *but*? Practice delivering the same message, using **'and'** instead of *but*. Imagine talking with your child or young person and replacing 'but' with 'and.' Notice the feelings. Imagine what it might feel like to be on the receiving end. Now, try it.

try this: Tell your child or young person that you will be trying to use 'and' versus 'but' and why. Ask for their patience and support and ask that they hold you accountable for it.

Scary? Yep.

Powerful? Just watch.

13

WHAT DO YOU WANT?

There I stood, halfway down the stairs, looking up at my seven-year-old son and ranting at the top of my lungs: *"How many times does it take? How many times do I have to say it before you actually get it?!"* (I'm not saying I was proud of my parenting at that moment, but I was *frustrated!*)

That memorable interaction came to a screeching halt when my son stamped his foot, pointed at me, and yelled, *"Dad, stop it!"*

In utter disbelief, I did just that. Then came the words that changed everything: *"Dad, don't tell me another thing you don't want me to do! Tell me what you do want me to do!"*

Tell me what you want me to do. How many times, in the craziness of our parenting and work, do we actually tell young people what we want from them? How often do we even know? The truth is, we want them to just *know* this great mystery on their own, to have the revelation themselves, to "get it" — and of course, for "it" to be exactly what we needed from them in the first place!

But the truth is, if I have to guess at what you want — other than knowing it's not what I'm currently doing — I'm left with only three options: risk the humiliation of being wrong, change nothing and hope for the best, or intensify my behavior in hopes of evoking clearer communication from you.

Sound familiar?

Over and over, young people have told me of the liberating impact of clear expectations. Not control, not rigidity — expectations, but a landmark by which I can tell where I am and where I want to go.

I may not meet your expectations, but knowing what they are helps me set my own.

———

reflect...

you: Think about situations with your child or young people in your life that you find particularly aggravating: dishes in a room, disruptions in the teen center, whatever. Do you know what you want? Is it negotiable? Can they do it? Could you state what you want (not what you *don't* want) in clear and precise terms? What is it?

try this: Bring one of these situations to mind. Say to your child or young person, "*I get pretty jacked up about this and it has occurred to me that I've never told you exactly what I need/want from you. I'm tired of what we've been doing and want to try something different. Let's make some agreements so I get what I need or want from you, and you can become more independent and don't have to feel harassed about it.*"

Now... improvise!

14

BUT SHE'S SO PASSIVE!

R ita is a smart, insightful, and bitingly funny girl of 16 — not that you would know it from talking to her. By her account, she's a talentless loser that no one likes.

And who could blame you for believing her? Each time you try to reflect her strengths, she bats it away with sarcasm — or worse, mean-spirited condemnation of your clueless observation skills. Rita is determined to be a passive player in her own life, refusing every invitation to consider a more positive perspective.

Familiar? Perhaps you've had a "Rita" in your life.

Is there anything quite as frustrating as trying to help someone who's given up on themselves? (*Though, let's be honest, she hasn't really given up — she's still actively debating with you about how she's a loser!*)

So, what do you do — *after* you remind yourself that your job is to do what's right, regardless of whether Rita gives you any reason to continue?

Well, perhaps you could focus your search for strengths on the very behaviors that drive you crazy! What about her incredible commitment to her own inaction? *It's called determination, willfulness, persistence, and tenacity.*

And you can't deny her creativity and cleverness when it comes to flipping every positive comment into self-deprecation. Sometimes, her sarcasm about your optimism is genuinely funny.

So, what do we do?

Two things seem to make the difference:

First, like a slow-dripping faucet, persistently tell her about these very strengths: *"Wow, you are a stubborn little sucker about being helpless, aren't you? I wish I was that tenacious in my life!"*

Or:

"That comeback was hilarious. I don't believe what you said is true, but that was very clever. You've got the gift, girl."

Second, affirm your belief in her ability to take action — even when she doesn't believe it herself: *"I get it that you don't think you can do it. I just want you to know that I know you can. When you're ready, I'll be here to cheer you on."*

In both approaches, persistence is key, for there's no greater testament than to have a young person say, *"You never gave up on me."*

"Never."

reflect...

you: Do you ever feel or act as stubbornly passive (or stubbornly anything) as Rita? What happens when others ignore this "manipulation" and speak directly to you, as if you were the strong and capable person that you are? Does it make you laugh? Does it make you angry? Do you want them to go away — and, at the same time, do you want them to stay? These are many of the reactions you can expect when you first "speak to the strengths."

them: Have you had someone like this in your life? What feelings did they evoke in you? Frustration? Annoyance? Anger? Pity?

Are there other kinds of kids who evoke similar feelings? Jot down some of the phrases you could use to stay "on message" with your intention to reflect strengths.

15

WHO BELIEVED IN RAY?

I remember the day the man I most wanted to be when I grew up died.

Ray Charles, my hero, went and died before I had a chance to meet him, to touch him, to speak to him.

As a child, I dreamed of being Ray Charles – free, soulful, completely out there. I practiced playing the piano with my eyes closed and imagined myself in front of crowds who couldn't get enough – just like Ray.

I tried again and again to rock back and forth without lifting my hands off the piano keys — like Ray could.

I longed for my joyful spirit to nearly leap out of my body the way Ray's did. I so wanted to not care what others thought, to be totally, foolishly, uninhibitedly me – just like Ray.

But I was cautious and followed the rules. I stood against the wall at the school dances. I was embarrassed often and rarely got into trouble.

My hero died... and this is what I know for sure:

Ray Charles' music touched me to the core, and if my life could have gone in any direction I could dream, I would play and sing like Ray. But the reason Ray Charles, the man, touched my soul was that he was absolutely authentic... sincere. Like my other hero, Leonard Bernstein, what you saw was what you got. No pretending, no fitting in, no playing by the rules. Ray did what he loved and did it with every delighted cell of his being. I'm not saying all this did not come without a cost to both my heroes and the people who cared for them, but as a child, it was this spirit of freedom that I saw and admired so.

Alas, I haven't Ray Charles' talent, nor his soul. I'm not blind. I didn't grow up poor and black in the South. I didn't watch my brother drown when I was five. I haven't the desire to seduce women as playthings, and I've never used cocaine.

I will never *be* Ray Charles.

But I can be authentic. I can choose to give voice to my soul. I can be unapologetic when I get excited or passionate, and my spirit is in flight and barely containable. I can fully give the world what I have to give.

And I can see in each young person that same unique, unbearably brilliant spirit.

Somebody saw it in Ray. And he became Ray Charles.

It could have been different, but he became Ray Charles.

Don't just blame it on the talent.

Somebody saw Ray... and helped open the door.

reflect...

you: What does it mean to you to be "authentic?" What does it look, sound, and feel like?

What would it feel like to acknowledge that authentic "you" each day?

Are you authentic with the young people in your life? If not, what would it look like if you were? What would it take to gain the courage to do so? Can you ask for that from friends, colleagues, or coworkers?

them: Name a young person in whom you can see that "unbearably brilliant spirit" that I referred to in this reflection. What would it look like to speak directly to that spirit?

What words would you use? What would you do differently? If they are living in difficult circumstances, how would you accomplish this in the midst of their chaos?

16

PARENTING IS LIKE JAZZ

I n my five decades of challenging work with children, youth, adults and organizations, no job has ever come even remotely close to the challenges and rewards of being a parent: the constancy of it, the deep, under-the-skin investment, and the messiness of it all.

Parenting has been like one long jazz improvisation:

Where I long to express an original idea instead of playing the same old tunes over and over.

Where I'm intuitively grabbing at the next chord just to keep pace with the music.

Where I'm trading solo time with my partner, but never fully leaving the stage (at least in my consciousness).

Where I'm alternating between moments of breathtaking beauty and awe — and stretches of feeling lost in the chaos of my own playing.

And always, *always* ready to try again — because the promise of finding just the right chord, just the right progression, is too wonderful to ignore.

As I began to pay attention to the richness of this analogy, here's what I noticed:

First, great jazz musicians know the unique and enduring strengths of each piece of music. They don't fight those qualities or bemoan that they aren't different. (Imagine complaining that *My Funny Valentine* isn't jazzy enough or that *Makin' Whoopee* isn't bluesy enough!)

Rather, they focus on, exploit, and playfully explore those strengths. They honor the strengths by amplifying them, enhancing them, and presenting them front and center. Oh, they know the flaws, but they also know that if they play to the strengths of the music — whether it be the rhythmic drive, the evocative melody, the clever lyrics, or the rich harmony — no one will notice those flaws. They know that a single piece rarely gets it all right — and who cares; they are too busy having fun with the heart of the music!

Second, I noticed that when great musicians play together, they are incredibly flexible and responsive to what each new moment brings. They're ready to shift, suggest a new direction, or go with the flow. It's often hard to tell who's leading and who's following. They bring this same respect for diversity, strengths, and sharing when they aren't soloing – delighting in what the other players can do that they cannot. They know they must count on each other's unique gifts.

Finally, they have a keen understanding of the underlying structure of each piece of music, and know the critical components that hold all music together: rhythm, tempo, melody, structure. They know that, without this foundation, all the rest would be just so much chaos.

Do we know what matters most with our kids? What's foundational, and what's free for improvisation?

Imagine if parenting could be both as grounded and as joyfully free as great jazz.

I invite you on a journey to explore how we can joyfully parent and mentor young people, joining the improvisation so they can know, grow, and live from their strongest selves.

———

reflect...

Share or jot down your reactions to this piece. What ideas resonated with you? Challenged you? Made you feel intrigued or interested?

In what ways have you tried to "parent by recipe," listening to what others said was right, even when your knowledge of your child told you differently? What do you "know" in your heart is right? What's holding you back?

What are we afraid will happen if we "play to the strengths?"

try this: In a group with other parents or professionals, share your experiences with "recipe parenting." Describe what was unique about your child that required a different approach? What did you do differently? What feelings or thoughts did you have that told you that you were on the wrong track? Share with each other what's scary about improvising with your children. Share with each other what feels strong or exciting or joyful about improvising with our children.

17

THE BOUNDARIES OF
IMPROVISATION

L et's take this jazz analogy to the next level, thinking about our teens.

To listen to a group of jazz masters, seasoned and mature, is to experience the miracle of exquisite improvisation that is seemingly built on the loosest of connections to the original tune. You can hear and feel the underlying *structure*, even as they explore the far reaches of what's possible. Yet, they always seem to know exactly how to get back home, where all is comfortably familiar, and we recognize that they were connected to it all along.

There is a constant tension between freedom and structure. Without that underlying structure, the improvisations drift into chaos and can't find their way back home. Without freedom, the music is staid and stiff and loses its soul.

Such is the independence we wish for the young people in our lives: adventurous *and* grounded; competent *and* connected; able to lose sight of the shore *and* always able to navigate back home.

A critical part of our role as adults is to provide this structure while fostering that freedom. Especially in the teen years, they want to be free *now*, masters of their world *now*. It is their job to push toward that end every day.

And it is our job to provide the resistance that tells them where "home" is. Success lies not in the chaos of being lost in their improvisation — as necessary as that is — but in their ability to find their way back to a place of equilibrium, safety, and groundedness.

This resistance tells them how long and how far they can explore, and how each new improvisation went. They know they aren't ready. They count on us to provide enough solo time to prove what they can do, but not so much that their explorations dissolve into chaos. It's just like the jazz masters, who earned and learned their 'chops' little by little.

Of course, we can't nurture future masters of life improvisation by following a script. We must improvise too!

We model the courage of acting on our own instincts: *"Yes, I get that you want to go to the party, but I love you, and I won't stand aside when I think you are in danger."*

We show them how to recover: *"I was wrong last night. You have earned the chance to show you can handle this. How can I support you?"*

We teach by example: *"I hear that you want to go out after the dance. And I need to know you are safe. How can we both get what we need?"*

Successful parenting improvisations require an intimate "knowing" of our kids. There are no shortcuts, and sometimes *we* may feel lost. But when we know our children — when we are listening and paying attention — we can fully engage in that terrifying and exhilarating daily improvisation that allows them to become jazz masters of their own lives:

Adventurous *and* grounded; competent *and* connected; confident and capable enough to lose sight of the shore *and* to navigate back home.

reflect...

you: Who helped you become a master of improvisation in your own life? How did they do it? If you didn't have someone, what was the impact of having no boundaries or guidance? What do you wish had been true?

them: When you set aside both your fear and your preconceptions about what is "correct," what are the "just right" boundaries for the young people in your life? How do you know? What conversations do you want to have with them and what do you want to ask? What do you want to negotiate?

What's true about your young person that impacts where the boundaries are? How can you honor the "knowing" of this child while still empowering them to learn how to make decisions and gain independence?

Where do you need to model courage?

Where do you need to model being accountable for mistakes?

Where do you need to teach by example?

try this: Look back at your answers to the last three questions. Picture yourself modeling this courage, accountability, and/or lesson. Hear yourself saying the words.

Now, try them out.

18

IN MY EYES: A STORY OF HOPE

O h, my sweet child. How I wish you could see yourself through my eyes.

Not my exhausted eyes,

that could barely keep up with you today,

but eyes filled with awe at your sheer persistence and will.

Not my anxious, ever-vigilant eyes,

that can barely breathe as I wait for yet another (always public) outburst or much-too-loud, and painfully inappropriate observation,

but eyes filled with wonder at the raw passion and energy of those meltdowns and the too-funny insight buried in those commentaries.

Not my exasperated eyes,

that sometimes want to give up after you've turned my world upside down yet again,

but eyes filled with admiration at the endlessly resourceful ways you seek to fill the empty spaces, ward off the gremlins, and make a connection that will upright your world.

Not my sad eyes

that grieve when you come home from school defeated by the struggle of it all,

but eyes filled with respect for your tenacity – and the resilience that will give rise to yet another day.

Not my fearful eyes,

that wonder how far you will go to see if I love you,

but compassionate, committed eyes that see your hurt

and long to wipe away any doubt.

Not my doubting eyes,

that wonder if I can even begin to give you what you need,

but eyes filled with honor and gratitude

for this chance to be in your life.

Oh, my sweet child.

How I wish you could see yourself through my eyes.

So, tomorrow I will strive once again

to be your alternate mirror,

where you can see the reflection of the *amazing surviving child* I see —

the persistent, passionate, insightful, funny, resourceful, resilient child you are.

Will you even glimpse in that mirror?

It's OK, I will stay until you see it...

In my eyes.

---

reflect...

you: Reflect on what touched you in this poem. Who did you think of as you read about this child? This parent?

What would it be like, as a child, to be seen in this loving way?

19

I NEED YOU MORE THAN EVER

Question to high school students: *"If your parents could understand only one thing from you, what would you most like them to know?"*

Answer: *"I need you now more than ever. I need you to stay engaged in my life, even though I reject you, act like I don't need you, and try to be as different from you as I can."*

Does the clarity of this message — *"I need you now more than ever"* — surprise you?

I'm not sure I would have ever discovered this truth had it not been for a group of teens at a high school in Maine. They were planning and facilitating a parent education workshop and had asked me to help.

So, I posed the question: *"If your parents could hear just one thing tonight, what would you most like them to know?"* I was so intrigued by their answer that I started asking this question of high school students everywhere I traveled across the US — hundreds over the course of many years.

Incredibly, this was the top response every single time I asked. (*Yes, I mean 100% of the time!*)

They didn't place *"Give me my freedom,"* or *"Trust me,"* at the top of their list. They said:

"Don't bail on me! I'm going to push the limits. I need to make my own decisions. You aren't going to like it sometimes. But please hold me accountable, talk to me about it, stay engaged."

It's a simple and deeply felt request — one that requires little elaboration or explanation. Those same kids, whose actions say, *"Stay away, I've already grown up,"* are actually saying, *"Please don't go away. I need you more than ever."*

As parents and other caring adults, this can feel like an awkward, frustrating, and terrifying minefield. How do we *not* react to the push-pull barrage of complaints? How do we *stay engaged* when we barely *see* our kids? How do we deal with our deep — and entirely reasonable — fears about the decisions they are making without us?

But now we know what's in their hearts. How can we not respond to their plea...

Please don't bail on me.

reflect...

you: Looking back on your own adolescence, can you resonate with this response? How did the most important adults in your life stay engaged while supporting your growth?

them: Think about the young people in your life. How do you see them asking for this — without asking for this! How do you navigate these waters? How do you stay engaged even as they push you away, both literally and metaphorically?

try this: Have this conversation with them. Share this story and ask them to reflect on it. Then, ask them what they most deeply want from you.

20

GIVE YOURSELF A BREAK!

Ok. First the disclosure: I'm not a big sports buff. I know just enough to be dangerous and have only rarely been known to utter a sports metaphor. However, all of life is a risk, so I will dare such a metaphor here.

I believe the biggest single barrier to focusing on strengths is fear — fear of getting it wrong (as if we're getting it right when we focus on deficits), and fear of the unknown and unfamiliar. Powerful enough on its own, when we combine fear with guilt and self-judgment, the mix is powerful enough to stop us in our tracks!

We know what we *want* to do, what young people *need* us to do, even what we're *inspired* to do; but because we can't manage to do it consistently, we walk around feeling defeated and guilty. We may feel like we're letting our children down or may beat ourselves up for not maintaining that positive, resilience-building perspective.

After a while, we tire of it all and return to our old patterns of trying to "fix" the deficits. At least we can do that consistently and well — even if it doesn't produce the results we want. And at least everyone is comfortable!

But here's the part we miss (and here comes the sports metaphor): Effective parenting (and youth work) is like baseball. If you're batting .300, you're a star!!

If 30% of the time we remember to notice, acknowledge, and teach young people about their strengths — even while holding them accountable for harmful behavior or naming expectations for different behavior – it's likely that we are giving them exponentially more than they are getting anywhere else.

And more good news: wait just a minute and you'll have another chance to do it right! That's right; they keep coming back for more!

Even better, just be sincere in the effort and get it right part of the time, and that's what they'll remember you for decades from now!

So this is my challenge: When you get it right, pat yourself on the back, have an extra chocolate, high-five your partner, colleague, or friend. And when you walk away shaking your head, having so competently focused on those deficits once again, laugh at your own foibles, grin at your persistence, and give an *"Oh well, there's always next time!"*

Why? Because kids (and all of us) are resilient! And because this self-aware lightness will allow you to stay focused on the next opportunity right in front of you.

Give yourself a break... 'cause three out of ten makes you a star!

reflect...

you: Do you ever find that you are beating up on yourself because you aren't doing this strengths-focused thing "well enough?" Describe the feelings and how it impacts your ability to parent or work effectively — and joyfully.

try this: Create a simple "success log." Each night, jot down at least three thoughts, decisions, or interactions that went well. When did you notice strengths, set healthy boundaries, or see through the clutter to what was happening *beneath* the behavior? Do this for 10 days and you'll find yourself doing these things more easily, more often, and more joyfully. Better yet, you'll stop beating up on yourself for the times when you didn't — because when you did, you changed their lives.

21

HIGH EXPECTATIONS... BUT WHOSE?

Day after day, week after week, year upon year, 16-year-old Aaron's parents, teachers, counselors, and well-meaning family friends have engaged in a futile, yet persistent, effort to get Aaron to join extracurricular activities, do his homework, improve his grades, and care more about his education.

After all, Aaron is a good-looking, sociable, and capable kid with a positive outlook on life. He's the kind of bright, competent kid who could probably succeed at just about anything he set his mind to.

He loves performing, composing, and creating. He plays in a garage band that has done a couple of gigs [*though they could do so much more if they just had a little discipline*]. He's been in a couple of school plays [*though he hasn't joined the Drama Club and isn't auditioning for the next one*] and he even wrote a new arrangement of the school song for the jazz band [*of which he is not a member*]. He's also a 'C' student — seemingly satisfied with that academic status — who is all too accustomed to seeing "does not perform up to his potential" on his report card.

Though his parents acknowledge that he has always "marched to a different drum," they fear for his future. Will he be disciplined enough, motivated enough, organized enough to succeed? As a result, Aaron's life with adults is defined mostly by what he is *not* doing: meeting their expectations.

So the battles persist and his parents feel the sting of their own guilt [*Have we failed him?*], as well as the subtle judgment of friends and neighbors [*Has he considered the armed services? My nephew was undisciplined, just like him, and...*].

Except for their neighbor, Fran. She thinks Aaron is awesome. Notice her awe. [*And the fears that so often prevent Aaron's parents and teachers from seeing him the same way*].

Fran envies Aaron's ability to listen to his heart and take the "road less traveled." [*But what about college? Not with those grades. And employers? They want you to march to their drum!*]

Fran loves Aaron's music. [*Then why doesn't he join the band? Do something with it?*] And she thought he stole the show in the school musical last year. [*Then why doesn't he commit to it?*]

Fran thinks Aaron will find a nontraditional way to get his education. [*But what if he doesn't?*] Perhaps he'll attend one of those funky schools that recruits creative kids just like him. [*A respectable college? With a degree that will get him a job?*]

Fran is confident that Aaron will find a creative way to make a living that fits his personality. [*But will he be able to support a family?*]

Most of all, Fran thinks Aaron will be happy.

Research tells us that having "high expectations" is an important part of being good parents and mentors. However, for expectations to be meaningful, they must be in sync with the child in front of us. What gets in the way is our fears, lurking in the wings, waiting to *own* these expectations — just so we don't have to feel so uncomfortable with the uncertainty of it all.

It is only when we name our own fears that we can step back and truly know and celebrate our children as separate and unique human beings — sometimes painfully different from ourselves, and our expectations.

When young people feel seen and honored for who they are, they can generously respond to our high expectations as an expression of our love and respect for them.

To be seen and honored for who they are... Isn't that what we *all* long for?

reflect...

you: What expectations did adults have for you when you were young? Were they a match for who you were and are? What would it have looked like, sounded like, and felt like to be seen and supported in this way?

them: Who are the "Aarons" in your life? What high expectations do you or others have for these young people? Are they aligned with who this person is? How will you know?

try this: Identify an "Aaron" in your life. Now, step into the role of Fran. See this young person through Fran's eyes? What would you say? What expectations would you have?

22

WHO'S IN A RUT?

"*She's such a bitch!*"

Thus began the latest tirade from a 15-year-old girl who always seemed to be at odds with her mother – and every other adult.

What followed was her standard litany of grievances: the latest unjust suppression of her "rights," the oppression of her creative spirit, and her mother's general determination to keep her from doing *anything*.

We had this same conversation countless times before, always with my requisite probing questions to help her pay as much attention to her own behavior as her mother's.

Today, I decided to try something different: I was determined to be quiet and see what she would do if I just listened – all the way – before saying anything.

This change in my response — or rather, lack of response — drew an immediate reaction:

"*What? What?*" she protested.

"I'm listening," I responded. *"Your mom's a complete bitch,"* I half-stated, half-asked.

"Well, yeah! You know how she is."

I could already hear her energy deflating — like a balloon with a slow leak. Her tirade lasted about two more sentences before she began to sputter and, to my surprise, take over *my* role in the conversation.

"I know she's just trying to protect me, but..."

"I guess I wasn't being so nice either, but she doesn't have to..."

"I just wish she wouldn't treat me like a little kid..."

"I guess maybe if I..."

By the time she finished, she had done what she'd never been able to do before — see her mom as the imperfect, struggling mom she was. She took responsibility for her part of the battle. And, remarkably, she began problem-solving ways to do it differently next time.

I was awed by her insight and wisdom — and stunned by how deeply she had internalized the very skills I'd tried to teach her in our previous conversations.

Why was I surprised? And why had it taken me so long to let her practice those skills on her own. Had my habitual response to her outbursts simply reinforced her old patterns? By listening — just listening — I had communicated, *"I trust you. You know what to do. You don't need me for this anymore."*

Clearly, it was *my* role that needed to change. The real question was: Was I ready?

Since that conversation, I have seen this pattern repeated over and over again. I had always seen the young people I worked with as being stuck in their habitual patterns of behavior. I guess they weren't the only ones.

How about you?

reflect...

you: Have you ever been in a rut like this with a young person? With yourself? Do you remember what got you out of the rut? Most likely, it was something unintentional that shook you out of your normal way of doing things. Can you go back and notice what you did differently — and what gave you the capacity to do so?

try this: Make a list of the young people you parent or work with. Put an asterisk beside each one with whom you engage in any repetitive conversations or interactions. Ask yourself: *"What do I get out of these interactions?"* (E.g. She gets to complain. I get to teach/coach.)

Now generate a list of the other ways you could react that would interrupt that old pattern. Put an asterisk by the ones that strike you as healthy, strong, or having promise. Try one out. Jot down what happened, what worked and what didn't?

try this: Next time you feel stuck or in a rut with a young person, just do something different – anything: tell a joke, go for a walk, play a game, tell a story, do something silly or crazy — anything to break the pattern. Not surprisingly, these are often the breakthrough moments when we get the results we've been striving for all along.

23

THE POWER OF ONE

"**K**urt," a high school senior, was living what felt like a vague, unreal nightmare. A good student and a highly responsible kid, he had lost the opportunity to apply for college scholarships when he found out his father hadn't paid taxes in many years and wouldn't risk completing the necessary forms.

Kurt soon quit each of his many extra-curricular activities so he could work after school. His father was drinking again. His mother was distracted and depressed.

His family was moving to a new town and he could smell the scent of long-threatened divorce in the air.

Passionate feelings for a new girlfriend were the one bright spot in his life.

All he cared about was graduating early and getting on with his life.

Needless to say, English class wasn't a priority — but it became his salvation. The teacher announced that each student was to maintain a daily journal of their thoughts, observations, favorite lyrics — whatever they wished. The journals would be turned in to her each Friday and returned each Monday.

What a pain!

Kurt didn't plan to spill out his feelings in that journal; it happened slowly. First, he shared just a little. On Monday morning, he found a few simple words of encouragement and empathy in the margins.

So he wrote a bit more. More words of support.

Soon, he could barely wait for Mondays to come. Trying to look nonchalant, he would immediately look to see what his teacher had written. Her words gave him courage and strength. It was like this private, magical world where Kurt could be passionate and angry and outraged — a world where, unlike home, there were no limits on what he could say or feel.

Perhaps that teacher had discussions with the school counselor or otherwise checked into Kurt's life, but he never knew. He just knew that journal was his oasis in a world where everyone seemed out of control.

That class lasted the requisite thirteen weeks (thirty-nine hours), and then Kurt moved, and it was over as quickly as it had begun.

Was it enough? Oh, it was more than enough. It was everything!

The impact of that teacher's simple act of seeing and honoring Kurt as the passionate, strong, struggling young man that he was has lasted a lifetime. He drew strength from those silent dialogues many times in his life.

That journal is yellowing now, and that teacher probably never knew the power of her words. I imagine she just did what she thought was right and hoped for the best.

What she did was save a life.

reflect...

you: Do you have anyone from your past with whom you had limited contact but who had an outsized impact on you? What would you say if you could talk to them today?

them: Is there a young person who may see you the same way?

try this: Write your own reflection, similar to the one here, about someone who had a great impact on you.

24

EVERYONE WINS

Being the noble "helpers" we are, we tend to discuss the benefits of a strengths-focus in terms of its benefits to the young people we serve.

Yet, as human beings, we tend to engage in behaviors that benefit ourselves.

Of course, those benefits can often seem paradoxical: We can be self-sacrificing because it makes us feel important. We can focus on deficits because it makes us feel more professional, more highly regarded, or even more competent. When we talk about burnout, it implies that we work harder and give more of ourselves than others. (*Heaven forbid we should be energized and delighted by our parenting or our work — who would take us seriously?!*)

So, it is with some trepidation that I suggest two *selfish* motivations for making the shift from deficits to strengths.

First, it makes us happier. It's more energizing to think about others as competent and to feel awed by their ability to survive. It's a relief to know that they managed to survive before we came along (making many mistakes, just as we do on our journeys) and that they have the perseverance to keep trying. We feel hopeful when we can see these incredible strengths, and it's more fulfilling to think that we could be the key to helping them recognize those strengths too!

Second, it works! We can see what happens when young people begin to think of themselves as survivors, instead of damaged goods; as remarkable instead of failures, losers, at-risk, or "troubled." Instead of the mind-numbing, *do-it-again-even-though-it-didn't-work-the-last-time* approach that blinds us to the unique and remarkable young people in front of us, we get to witness slow but steady progress as they experiment with the strengths we have shown them in the "alternate mirror."

We can feel the rise of hope and energy in them, and that, in turn, energizes us.

Make no mistake; it's still hard work (harder, if you ask me). But when that hard work is also energizing, awe-inspiring, hopeful, and fun, then we are happier. And when we are happier, we are better parents, better professionals, better people!

So, you can focus on strengths because you are noble and caring, striving to be the most effective parent or professional you can be, or you can focus on strengths because it results in a happier, more relaxed, and satisfied you.

Either way, it seems to me that everyone wins.

reflect...

you: Can you relate to the sentiments in the first paragraph? Share or jot down your reflections on this.

Have a conversation about what it feels like to choose to focus on strengths; to be awed instead of annoyed, to be hopeful.

Share ways you have witnessed the impact of focusing on strengths.

try this: Write down and/or declare to a partner or group your decision to focus on strengths because it's better for you (e.g. *"I choose to focus on strengths because it makes my job easier and more fun, makes me feel lighter and more joyful, and because I like results!"*)

25

THE ART OF BREAKING THE RULES

" T amara" is no one's favorite. She thinks adults are power-hungry, untrustworthy and absolutely clueless — and in her life, they often have been. Teachers cringe when she walks into class with her defiant eyes and belligerent attitude. Every behavior, every word seems designed to give the finger to the status quo. Adults experience a barely disguised combination of disgust and genuine fear when dealing with Tamara, and she knows the power she wields.

Her latest? Wearing a dramatic black and red T-shirt with a blatantly violent message emblazoned across the chest.

While Tamara sulked through her first few days in the alternative program for "behaviorally challenging" kids, she rose a bit to the challenge of playing hard-core basketball with a menagerie of misfit peers and staff. When she then volunteered to participate in a service project, staff members were proud and delighted. They risked an inkling of hope as they watched Tamara walk away with her box of supplies. Only when they left for the day did they discover her spray-painted handiwork all over the back wall of the building.

Decision point: Should Tamara be immediately dismissed from the program, as outlined in the behavioral agreement? Logic and consistency say *"yes."* Something inside Jade, the lead teacher, said *"no,"* and she convinced the principal to let her try to keep Tamara connected to the program.

Tamara arrived the next day prepared to be sent home — or rather to her regular hangouts — and was shocked to find Jade waiting with all the supplies needed to clean the building.

For the next few hours, she did her requisite ranting, cursing, and sulking. But, remarkably, she completed the job. Jade then matter-of-factly informed Tamara that they would never speak of the incident again, nor would she tell anyone what had happened.

Since that day, Tamara has completed the program, returned twice to do service work, and has asked to be appointed to a special youth board.

So, did Jade do the right thing? Did he give Tamara, who had signed the behavioral agreement, a mixed message? Couldn't this have been a waste of precious time and resources? (Answer key: Depends on your perspective. Yep. Absolutely.)

So what do we take from this? Is there something to learn here or did Jade just get lucky?

I doubt luck was the key factor here. More likely, years of truly *knowing* kids gave Jade a strong sense of what was "right" in this situation. She understood the importance of consistency with these kids — and I suspect she knew exactly what she would do if Tamara refused to take responsibility for her actions.

She also knew that resilient kids tend to be those who have heard this message from an adult they trust: *"You matter. It doesn't matter what you have done before. I believe in you."*

Her years of hard-earned wisdom gave Jade the confidence to listen to her well-informed gut and take the chance that she was right. She improvised. But like any good improviser, she knew where she was, where she was going, and how to get back home.

The result? Tamara glimpsed an alternate view of herself — and decided to live up to it.

This is art.

reflect...

you: Did you have any experiences like this when you were growing up—or even as an adult? Reflect on how it felt to be given that second chance, to have someone break the rules so that you could succeed.

them: Think about times when doing what you thought would be most effective for a young person meant breaking (or bending) the rules. If you took the risk, how did that feel to you? Were there consequences for you? And how did you defend your actions?

try this: Without committing to any action, think about ways you might like to respond to a young person that might require you to bend the rules. What impact do you think this would have on them? Is there a way to make this safe for you and them? What you do next is up to you. No judgment. No "shoulds." Just walking through this exercise will make you more available to them.

26

AUDACIOUS ACCOUNTABILITY

I f you're reading this book, you're likely a caring and empathetic person. When you witness a young person struggling because of behaviors they've developed in response to lousy circumstances that are out of their control — alcoholic parents, failing schools, neighborhoods riddled with violence and fear, hopelessness — it may feel terribly unfair to hold them accountable in the same way you would others. But consider this: the sense of power and control that comes with taking 100% responsibility — not for events and circumstances, but for your *response* to those events and circumstances — can be incredibly liberating and empowering.

This is at the heart of "audacious accountability:" the process of loving, supporting, and affirming the strengths in young people, while simultaneously holding them accountable for their words and actions.

I have done few things more powerful and empowering, few things that generated as much maturity, growth, and stability in young people, than giving them the experience of audacious accountability.

When I ran a teen center, my office was often the final repository of conflicts. There were always two sides to the story and two parties that had been wronged. Both parties, of course, would insist that, if the other hadn't _____ (fill in the blank), there would be no problem in the first place. Both were very clear that it was the other person's fault — and they wanted to know what *I* was going to do about it, damnit!

I would bring each one — alone — into my office to tell their story. I cared not one bit about who was right or who was at fault — and they knew that.

Once they had done their tap dance about the unfairness of it all, they knew what I would require: that they tell me, without ever mentioning the other person's name or behavior, about *their* role in whatever had gone down. Though they would try valiantly to get me to talk about the other person and what I was going to do about their behavior, they knew it was all in vain. They knew that I would not tell them the consequences meted out to the other person, nor would I ever tell the other person theirs. We would talk about the strengths and insights they brought to bear on the situation. And we would talk about the consequences for their behavior.

This sometimes took quite a long time. One evening, I sat across from a young man who really struggled with this process. Each time he veered off course and began to talk about the other kid, I would stop the conversation and ask him to begin the story again. About 35 minutes and a dozen reboots into our meeting, he once again failed to stay focused on his response. I dramatically fell out of my seat and sprawled onto the floor. Looking up at him, I whined, *"You're killin' me here!"*

He laughed at my Oscar-winning performance and we began again. A couple tries later, he did it. He told the entire story without blaming, and he took full responsibility for *his* role in the conflict. While he rolled his eyes in mock disgust, I whooped and hollered, and we did a high-five.

As he walked out of my office, he looked at his offending friend — who had been waiting for his turn — and said, *"Watch out, he'll wear you out in there!"*

What was so rewarding was the pride in his voice as he said it. I could almost hear his inner thoughts: *"Man, he must really care about me!"* and *"No one can hurt me; I'm in control of me."*

I saw this look often over the years, and, with many, it wasn't long before *they* began to lead our conversation through these steps. *They* began to claim their right to "audacious accountability." And *they* began to talk about how they wanted to respond to the real adversity in their lives.

They had been held accountable and it felt strong and right and powerful.

Audacious.

reflect...

you: Can you think of a time when you blamed others to avoid taking 100% responsibility for your response to an event or circumstance? How did that feel? Was there a point when you were able to take "audacious responsibility?" How did that feel? Do you think this might be true for the young people in your life, as well?

them: Are there young people in your life who, faced with unfair circumstances, spend all their time and energy explaining why it wasn't their fault — and wondering what you're going to do about it?

try this: Thinking about this young person, imagine the kind of conversation I've described. It may be your own version, in your own style, but a conversation where they can name their part, completely separate from anyone or anything else there is to blame. Try it out — not expecting perfection the first time out, but determined to master the art of empowering young people in this way.

27

DO YOU BELIEVE?

I remember the day I spent on a beautiful island with my daughter, exploring and building fairy houses with three 10-year-old girls. We imagined the fairies coming out at dusk and delighting in their new homes and playgrounds. We were careful to design each element 'just so,' so the future tenants would be pleased. Our delight at imagining what might happen when we weren't looking was absolutely contagious!

This wonderful energy was evoked by fairies that probably don't even exist! (*Though I'm not positive of that.*) It made me wonder why we don't experience the same energy when we do what we know is right for the young people in our lives — without knowing if it will "work." We create safe and sacred places for them, reflect their strongest selves back to them, and help them put in context the challenges they face each day.

Yet, instead of delighting in what these actions might make possible long after we are there to bear witness, we look for "V-8 moments," when they slap their foreheads and tell us we have done it right, *we've changed their lives!*

We can't wait for dusk; *we want results right now!*

Make no mistake about it: working with young people requires our most "adult" selves, setting aside instant gratification for long-term gain. But we can remember how the important people in our lives changed our lives. We have read the research, heard the stories, and seen with our own eyes what happens when just one person is fully present, aware, and engaged in the life of a young person. Yet, too often, building fairy houses can evoke more faith in a mysterious future than what we have experienced ourselves and seen in others.

So try this: At the end of your day today, think of just one moment when you were fully present, aware, and engaged with a young person. Revel in that moment. Delight in its power. And imagine that you have added another brick to the foundation of that young person's life. Do this every day and you may find tiredness turning into delight and wonder.

If you can believe in fairies, which you haven't seen, surely you can believe in your own power to change lives, which I *have* seen.

reflect...

you: Who are the people from your past who may not know the positive impact they had on your life? What was their impact? What did they do? Were you aware that they might have been doubting their own influence on your life?

try this: First, imagine telling the adults you referred to above how important they were in your life and why. What would you say to them? Now, pretend a young person in your life has come back after ten years to tell you how important you were.

What are they saying?

Now, go back and read the daily practice described in the next-to last paragraph of this reflection.

That.

Do that.

28

THE MISSING PIECE

I am grateful to my brother, James, for sharing this extraordinary story about his 6th-grade teacher, Mrs. Bergeron, at J.C. Knight School in Jonesboro, Indiana, circa 1963. Used with permission.

Does anyone remember Mrs. Bergeron? She was the imposing older farm woman who taught 6th grade. The view out her classroom window looked over empty fields. She looked like she could hurt a cow if it came to a disagreement. Nobody tested her.

She taught the 20 kids sitting in front of her every day. That's what she did.

We showed up. That's what we did. But she also worked for my higher power – quietly, anonymously, without a conscious invitation.

I remember the day of the SRT tests. Reading. Comprehension. School. Stuff that lacked meaning to me. Taking these tests gave me the fidgets.

My twin brother sat in the room a floor below me doing the same thing. I'd been passed forward — a failing student — to dodge the shame of graduating a different year from my twin. I'd been told I was slow, so I kind of knew my station in that class of kids who'd heard the same.

A few days after the test, Mrs. Bergeron moved me to the front of the class and asked, *"Can you see the chalkboard?"* Odd question, I thought, but the answer was, *"Yes."* The day before, it would have been, *"No."* (*How did she know? I didn't.*)

Then, she told me, *"You have a gift that's ready to open."*

I remembered my 5th-grade teacher, who had no problem writing an F on everything I did. And here was Mrs. Bergeron, talking to me as if those Fs weren't me.

At the end of the first grading period, she gave me an A. So did Mr. Richter across the hall, and the new math teacher downstairs. What was going on here? Why had the universe changed?

At the end of that year, Mrs. Bergeron told me I was her only student who tested at a high school level in reading comprehension. Then, she hugged me.

That hug was the missing piece. I felt like I had met God, and I would never forget it.

Anybody else have a day like that?

———

reflect...

you: Have you ever had a teacher like Mrs. Bergeron? What did that person see that others had not?

them: Whether you are a teacher or parent or other caring adult, how could you be a Mrs. Bergeron to the young people in your life? What would that look like—for you, in your style?

try this: Think about one young person in your life whose sense of self might be altered by the way you see them, speak to them, or regard them? What do you see that they have not yet seen? Now, decide on one way you can let them in on this secret about themselves.

29

TRUST THE RADAR

What does it feel like to feel cared for? Some years ago, at a greasy spoon in southwestern Ohio, I discovered the answer to that question.

Across from me sat "Diz," a high school teacher I hadn't seen in more than 30 years. In my memory, Diz was one of the good ones — those ever-present teachers and mentors who know how to connect with the kids in their class.

But he was much more to me. The disaster that was my home life during my high school years was a well-kept secret.

At school, I was a good student, an uber-responsible kid absorbing all I could from teachers and mentors like Diz — without blowing my cover.

But why was Diz in my life? He wasn't one of my teachers — at least, not yet. And I wasn't just benignly benefiting from an adult who just happened to cross my path. Where did he come from?

Over our second cup of coffee, I learned that Diz had chaperoned a choir trip I had been on. Despite my well-rehearsed facade, he recognized something in me: the look of a kid in pain, a kid with secrets and challenges being managed in the shadows.

He decided, he told me over pancakes, to simply make himself available to me.

"You mean you reached out to me on purpose?" I asked.

"In a way," he nodded. *"I didn't really do anything different. I just stayed aware of you and decided I would be available to you if you needed me."*

Can you imagine how, as a kid with secrets, my "radar" had locked onto that signal? For reasons I can't explain even now, I started leaving the building by a different door — the one near his classroom. I'd glance in the door as I walked by, hoping, I imagine, to be noticed.

One day he called out to ask my opinion on a page layout for the yearbook. He was the advisor. Soon, I was on the yearbook staff, spending endless hours in that incredibly safe space.

Can you imagine how it felt, sitting across from him some 20 years later, to learn that this lovely man — who I thought was just being a good guy, a happy accident — had seen through my bravado and purposefully decided to "make himself available" to me?

It felt like a life ring then. It fills me with gratitude now. Someone saw me and reached out — quietly, respectfully, expecting nothing — on purpose.

This is the opportunity available to us each day: not to solve problems, fix what's wrong, or dramatically change the world, but to see through the clutter, send out the signal that we "see" someone, and "trust the radar."

Who saw you?

Who will you see today?

———

reflect...

you: Did you have a "Diz" in your life? What did this look like? How did your radar align with their intention to care for you? What was their impact on the way you saw yourself, and how did this impact you as you grew into an adult?

them: Are there young people in your life who evoke a special sense of caring and concern? Describe what this feels like and how you've interpreted this feeling?

try this: How would you like to quietly make yourself available to this young person, on their terms and their timeline. Without any attachment to the outcome, hold this intention clearly and allow yourself to simply notice — and respond.

30

SIMPLE SHIFT, BIG RESULTS

A recent conversation with a mom reminded me once again of the transformative power of simple shifts in thinking. She had been struggling with her adolescent son who — right on schedule — was experimenting with his behavior, choice of friends, limits, and more. Mom was understandably and rightfully concerned. She spent significant energy tracking where he was, who he was with, and what he was doing.

She spoke (complained?) to him about his behavior and why she was concerned about his current choices. *Isn't this what she was supposed to do? Isn't this what the parenting books, and the counselors at school, and those "Where are your kids?" commercials on TV said to do?* So why did she end up feeling more like a stalker than a caring and responsible parent?

I'm not sure if any one event prompted the shift, but she could feel her relationship with her son slipping away and decided that this was no way to live — for either of them. So she sat down with her son to share her love and her concerns. Then, she outlined what was OK in their family and what was not, and was clear about the consequences if he chose to engage in the latter. She let him know that she recognized the reality that, in the end, these were going to be his decisions.

She could not control his every thought and action, but she could love him and try to help him be safe.

The result? A conversation. A more relaxed and less anxious Mom. A son who seemed to be around more, joined her for errands, and chatted about nothing and everything. She felt like the heart connection with her son had been renewed and she understood that it was this connection that was going to help keep him safe.

Mom is still paying attention to who, what, and where, but with a different intention and a different heart. They are both happier, more relaxed, and more connected. Their relationship feels solid and dependable, and less at risk of falling apart.

Is this particular shift right for everyone? Probably not. Some kids need stronger boundaries and monitoring, some need less; some relationships have been strained for too long for this conversation to work, and some families have too many other stressors to find room for this quality of relationship. But there is certainly a lesson to be learned from this very wise and insightful mom. She took the time (and trusted herself) to question the parenting recipes, and improvised a response that was right for her.

The shift was subtle, more about attitude than action.

The results were profound.

reflect...

you: How do you wish adults in your life had better understood what would work for you? What would you like to tell them — and if you could rewrite the script, what would be different?

them: Think about the young people in your life. What are the little shifts in your thinking that might shift the way they respond to you?

try this: Put this into action. How will you speak and act differently with them? With no expectations, try. Adjust. Experiment. See if you can align with the way this young person functions in the world. And imagine how it will feel to them to be seen in this way.

31

FIVE THINGS I LEARNED FROM RESILIENT KIDS

"I've never said, 'Why me?' That's life. I try to keep a positive attitude. If you start feeling sorry for yourself, that's when it gets bad." ~Rick Schwartz

Over the course of 30 years, I worked with kids of every description: profoundly delayed preschoolers, language-delayed children, institutionalized kids, teens who were natural leaders, high-risk teens, and more.

No matter the challenge, I was constantly blown away by their sheer resilience and spirit. Everything I teach, write, and speak about has its roots in what I learned from those kids.

Here are five things those kids knew — and the rest of us could learn from. (Isn't it fascinating that researchers and thought leaders are coming to the same conclusions as these resilient young people?)

Lesson 1

No matter how much I stare at, curse, talk about, or bemoan my lousy circumstances, there is some stuff I just can't control — and it's not worth my time trying. It's best to focus on what's next.

Lesson 2

I'm way, way stronger than I think I am — and it pays to remember that.

Lesson 3

I'm still standing on two feet. That means something. And it's worth figuring out how I did it.

Lesson 4

When you're "weird" — whether that means poor, overweight, "slow," awkward, ugly, out of place, or whatever — it's best to just be who you are. It saves a lot of time and grief, and people are more likely to think you are "good-weird" instead of "weird-weird!"

Lesson 5

It's not that hard to tell whether someone has good intentions or not. Trusting my instincts saves a lot of time and energy. When your gut tells you not to trust someone — listen.

reflect...

you: What lessons did you learn from your own adolescence? How do they inform your life today?

try this: Try asking the young people in your life what lessons they have learned and what wisdom they have gained from their life experiences? Be genuinely grateful and in awe of the lessons they have to teach you. Let them know how much you value their insights.

32

THE ONES WE LOSE

ften, at some point in a presentation, I am asked about "the ones we lose"— a reference to young people who continue to struggle mightily, despite the best efforts of caring adults. It's a question that weighs heavily on the minds of those who work with kids whose lives are in chaos.

To find the answer, I invite the audience to consider their own lives.

Do you still engage in negative choices or behaviors that no longer serve you? I ask. Perhaps your struggles are around food or lifestyle or relationship — or just about that persistent negative self-talk that keeps you from living the life you imagined.

Despite knowing better, despite countless "aha" moments of clarity about why you do it and what you want to do differently — and even with the support of people who love you — you hang onto these 'maladaptive' thoughts and behaviors.

Are you a lost cause? A slow learner? Or is this just the

journey you need to take before you can see and choose a new path?

What would it take for you to do things differently? Is there a magic bullet — something "perfect" that someone else could do or say that would change everything? Or would you, even then, need to find your own way?

And so it is with young people.

Though you may feel great sadness, loss, or anxiety about their choices (just as you may about your own), you may have already changed their lives. They may simply need more time to internalize their strengths, believe the alternate mirror you've shown them, or risk the losses that come with any change.

So, you do what you know helps: You name and honor their strengths. You offer resources, support, and love. You walk alongside them instead of trying to fix them.

And when they reject what you offer (for now) or you can no longer be in their lives, you silently bless them and hold onto your belief that they can find their own way.

You give them a light they can carry with them and draw on when they are ready to see it.

Ask any young person who has been down this longer, scarier road, and they will tell you exactly who believed in them, who offered an alternate mirror, and who was on their mind when they were finally ready.

We are just visitors on their path, characters in their story. Characters can be life-changing, but they aren't in charge of the story.

We are where we are — never lost, always on the way, always seeking to self-right, always looking for that alternate mirror that shows us what we can't yet see. That journey is why we are here.

Some stories are harder to witness and harder to live than others, but we are never truly lost.

reflect...

them: Are there — or have there ever been — young people in your life whom you felt you couldn't reach? Reflect on how that feels. What are the thoughts you have about them that have led to this feeling? Do you know them to be true?

try this: Imagine what you are not able to see or know — times when they made different decisions or moved through challenges with a bit more ease because of you. And imagine a day in the future when some words of encouragement from you, some memory of how it felt to be seen, or some recognition of a strength you showed them might take root and grow.

33

SAYING GOODBYE WELL

Over the years, I've said goodbye to a great many young people as I pursued more interesting challenges, escaped lousy working conditions, or adapted to changes in my own life. It always felt unfair to leave them. They had endured so many losses, been abandoned so many times — and in so many ways. Didn't they deserve better than to have me do the same?

I suspect this is why so many of my co-workers would promise kids that they would "stay in touch" after they moved on. (Of course, they never did, nor would it have been particularly healthy for them to have done so.) Alternatively, they assured kids that all would be well, and that it really wasn't a big deal.

But it seemed to me that the part we needed to get right was how to leave well; providing these young people with perhaps their first experience with a "healthy" goodbye.

I began to view each departure as a rich opportunity for growth — a "teachable moment."

This took many forms. Here's one:

When I left a stint as the director of a teen center, I bought a large piece of soft lamb's wool fabric and cut it into two-inch squares. On each square, I ironed the words:

"You are strong. You are resilient. You are loved."

As part of a goodbye ritual I did with each of the "regulars" at the center, I talked about the courage and strength I had witnessed in them during our time together. As I gave each one a piece of the fabric, I talked about how safe, secure, and loved a baby feels when wrapped in a soft blanket and held by a loving adult. I knew — as did they — that most of them hadn't had this life-affirming experience. I encouraged them to keep this piece of "baby blanket" so they could remember that, during our time together, they experienced moments of feeling safe, secure, and loved. I told them that the memory of those moments could give them courage and strength when times were tough.

Now, I'm no fool. I knew that many of those swatches would end up in the trash before the day was out. However, two years later, I ran into a young man who had challenged me at every turn during my time at the center. His life seemed like one big, endless struggle.

From a half-block away, he started yelling my name. *"Hey, Chris!"* I wasn't sure what to expect.

As he ran up to me, he pulled that piece of fabric out of his pocket.

"I still have it!" he said. *"It works."*

---

reflect...

you: What experiences have you had with saying goodbye — as the person leaving? As the person being left?

What worked, and what hurt?

try this: Imagine that you have gotten a promotion, new job, or other opportunity that causes you to leave your current work with young people. How can you say goodbye in a way that strengthens them? (Not take away the sadness, just strengthen the result.) Is there anything you want to change now that will enhance that healthy goodbye later?

34

THANK YOU, MISTY

My friend Misty lived in dozens (yes, dozens) of foster placements before she was 18 years old. She faced more adversity, more random and unfathomable pain, than a child should ever have to endure. She acted out — yes, she was one of *those* kids — and gave it right back to the world: angry and entitled.

Then, with a contagious smile that lit up every room she entered, she got her master's degree in Social Work and set about changing the world, especially for children — and the adults they would become — who hadn't been held precious in the way every child deserves.

She changed their world in big and meaningful ways. She built a national organization that attracted the support of celebrities and made the unseen feel seen and known — all through her indomitable spirit.

In her 30s, her body was ravaged by a disease that put her behind a walker when she should have been enjoying the fruits of her success.

Still, her smile lit up the world.

Then, before midlife, came early-onset Alzheimer's. (*What?!*) Even then, her light refused to be extinguished. She brought us along on the journey with her, sharing Facebook posts like *"the 10 best things about Alzheimer's"* (e.g., you can enjoy the same episode of your favorite sitcom like it's the first time every time). She filled her days — and her mind — with beautiful, intricate drawings.

Now, as her physical body prepares to leave this world much too early, my heart breaks and bursts with joy at the same time.

Misty, you are one of the brightest lights my world has ever encountered. Ray Charles, Nelson Mandela, the Dalai Lama... these are bright lights I never got to meet.

But I got to meet you.

I remember when, three days into our first encounter in the redwood forests of Southern California, surrounded by kids in foster care, you told me I was the first person ever to spend that much time with you without asking to hear your story — by which you meant your well-known, oft-repeated adversity story.

I looked at you and said, *"Misty, I have YOU, right here. I can see your light. What else do I need to know?"*

We all so deeply want the excuse of our adversity — an explanation for being less than who we really are. Misty taught us to claim our adversity stories, but not to live in them. She taught us that what we do next is always a choice. And she taught us that we are so much more than we ever imagined.

Our strength comes from our adversity. The expression of that strength comes from choosing a new story.

Thank you, Misty, for showing us how.

R *eflect...*
Just that. Reflect.

35

LIFE'S LITTLE MIRACLES

I have come to believe in miracles...

Or, little gifts, really — presented like life rings in the midst of disaster.

You see, my mother was sad.

Always trying to kill herself.

Always trying to make sense of a past (and present) that made no sense.

I was born to make her happy... and keep my father married to her.

I made her proud,

kept her company,

listened to her secrets,

and kept away the silence.

She never knew me separate from that purpose.

Yet, in the midst of that craziness, I was given these little gifts of being well-loved.

Like Corky — wonderful, gravelly-voiced Corky, who worked in the shoe department at the behemoth department store in downtown Fort Wayne. While my mother shopped, I would play at Corky's side or under the mile-high counter as she waited on customers. How was it that I was never in the way? During the breaks, Corky would pull me up into her lap as I recited my latest rhymes and cracked her up with a hundred knock-knock jokes. She was my ever-appreciative and never-satiated audience of one. When I was with Corky, I was the very best and only – and vice versa!

And there was Charlotte: an odd, overweight woman of unknown age, with missing teeth, a young son, and a mother who lived with her. That was their family. They looked poor, talked loud, frequently used the wrong words, and, unlike my family, did nothing to try to look any different than they were.

Oh, yeah, and Charlotte was really happy. Nearly all the time. And she loved kids, even me — a way-too-serious, hiding-my-secrets teenager! She made me do crazy things and didn't care when I soaked her with the hose at the car wash. I secretly admired her more than just about anyone I knew — very secretly, for she was the butt of many jokes at my house. But I knew she was better than us — 'cause at my house I couldn't breathe, but when I was with Charlotte, it was like my lungs opened right up and gulped down the freshest, happiest air I had ever known.

And even the good days with my mother, when we would take long drives in the car (it didn't matter where), still evoke a deep longing in me. There was our predictable stop for hot chocolate and "grown-up" conversation and our shared delight every time "our song" came on the radio. And, as dusk lowered the shades, I would curl up on the seat next to her, my head in her lap and the low rumble of the road escaping beneath me as she hummed in her rich, deep alto voice. That sound — no, that sensation — vibrated through my body as if the angels themselves had come from the depths of the warm earth and wrapped their arms around me.

So the little gifts are given.

In the confusion of craziness, in the midst of disaster, help always comes.

It can seem fleeting for sure, but help always comes.

And we survive.

And we remember.

And we thrive.

reflect...

you: What feeling reaction did you have to this reflection? Write these reactions down and share them.

If you grew up "in the midst of disaster," what were the moments of "being well-loved?"

How did/do these moments sustain you? Sit quietly and experience the feelings of caring, hope, being seen, or other feelings associated with it. What went right?

try this: Write your version of "Life's Little Miracles" or write one as you imagine a young person in your life might. How do they write about you?

ABOUT THE AUTHOR

Chris Trout has explored the nature of human resilience for nearly 50 years. Founder of *Strengths in Focus* and, more recently, *Lead Differently LLC,* his teachers have been an endless stream of resilient youth, adults, and organizations who have faced adversity and not only survived, but thrived. In 2005, after 27 years of in-the-trenches work in education and social services, Chris moved onto the national stage to inspire diverse audiences — from teachers in inner-city Los Angeles to mentors in rural Canada. His writings extended that reach around the world, engaging professionals from New Zealand to South Africa. A lover of fascinating people and transformative ideas, Chris continues his work as a speaker, consultant, writer, and coach from his home on the coast of Southern Maine.